An Introduction to Syncromysticism

Understanding the Generative Principle

William Anthony Ortiz

ISBN: 978-1-63263-961-5

Published by Abuzz Press, St. Petersburg, Florida, U.S.A.

Printed on acid-free paper.

Library of Congress Cataloguing in Publication Data
Ortiz, William Anthony
An Introduction to Syncromysticism by William Anthony Ortiz
Religion | Philosophy | Body, Mind & Spirit
Library of Congress Control Number: 2017942636

Abuzz Press
2017

First Edition

DISCLAIMER

This book details the author's personal experiences with and opinions about mysticism. The author is not a licensed Sorcerer.

The author and publisher are providing this book and its contents on an "as is" basis and make no representations or warranties of any kind with respect to this book or its contents. The author and publisher disclaim all such representations and warranties, including for example warranties of merchantability and financial advice for a particular purpose. In addition, the author and publisher do not represent or warrant that the information accessible via this book is accurate, complete or current.

The statements made about products and services have not been evaluated by the U.S. government. Please consult with your own legal, accounting, medical, or other licensed professional regarding the suggestions and recommendations made in this book.

Except as specifically stated in this book, neither the author or publisher, nor any authors, contributors, or other representatives will be liable for damages arising out of or in connection with the use of this book. This is a comprehensive limitation of liability that applies to all damages of any kind, including (without limitation) compensatory; direct, indirect or consequential damages; loss of data, income or profit; loss of or damage to property and claims of third parties.

You understand that this book is not intended as a substitute for consultation with a licensed medical, legal or accounting professional. Before you begin any change your lifestyle in any way, you will consult a licensed professional to ensure that you are doing what's best for your situation.

This book provides content related to mystical topics. As such, use of this book implies your acceptance of this disclaimer.

Dedication

This book is dedicated to my daughter Skye Trinity, and to my son Alexander Magnus. The Eternal Soul knows, it is the gift of love, that sparks the fires of creation.

Table of Contents

Chapter I

The Eternal Consciousness

With the onset of the 21st century, and the possibilities of humanity looking simultaneously, both very exciting, and seemingly dark and ominous, many people are seeking out new ways to come to terms with the direction of their lives. Old ways and ideas continue to persist in the minds of a population that is becoming increasingly marginalized in all aspects of their own personal lives. The realities of modern life have led to new personal and societal problems.

We now have less control over our everyday experiences and expenditures than ever before. As technologies advance, and government power continues to grow at the expense of the working classes, many people have given up on the realization that they can control their own lives and create a better future for themselves and their offspring.

There most certainly is a disconnect between the haves and the have-nots, about what is the best way to assure a better way.

The future of life, for both humanity and the multitude of species that inhabit this world we share, have reached a critical moment in time. Differences of opinion, and alternative philosophies, have long been a part of any civilized society. Mostly these things have a way of working themselves out, but not always to the satisfaction of both parties, let alone one side. What seems to be certain, today, is that the divide between the two visions for the future of our global technological civilization is as wide as the skies.

Utopia or dystopia, if one thing is for sure, it's that technology is going to play a big part in the future comfort, and discomfort of humanity. We will rule it, or it will rule us, and it doesn't have to be sentient to do it. Artificial Intelligence has been redefined as a classification for a program that takes the decision making away from human beings. Although, contrary to popular opinion, consciousness for machinery is a mere fantasy. Only the mind can distinguish itself from the universe.

The programming will get better, but if the object is to control the population in the same way that the current system is set up to do so, then the result will surely be human bondage for all. It often takes a certain amount of violence and spilled blood before people are willing, or able, to see the futility of human subjugation. Somehow, though, despite all the millennia of human history and conflict, and the near universal condemnation of it, slavery continues to exist.

Some certainly prefer serfdom to war or starvation. Some even welcome the stability of slavery to the uncertainty of self determination and free will. I, on the other hand, and many like me, have come to realize that the current system of economic enslavement is both, completely amoral, and ultimately unsustainable. There are real problems with the way that the governments around the world rule tyrannically over their own citizens, while simultaneously implementing the directives of the international banking powers.

There doesn't seem to be anything that money can't buy today. That is if you can get your hands on some. Karl Marx famously stated that all capital comes from labor, and he may have been correct at the time, but that just isn't the case anymore. The power to create and control the distribution of capital now lies in the hands of but a few powerful families and institutions, and they use it ruthlessly to achieve their goals of global domination.

You may ask how any of this is related to Syncromysticism, but I think you may have already figured it out. It is simply a matter of control. Some people may believe that the course of human history is an accidental hodgepodge of men muddling through it all, and trying to create a better way of accomplishing the things that they desire to do. It is true that these are the things most people do, but their goals and ambitions are so shortsighted, that they are easily overthrown, or usurped, by those who scheme ruthlessly to subjugate humanity, and to serve their own selfish desires. If it was just a matter of individual prowess, or simply the consequences of more vs less. Then the many citizens, would come out ahead of those few who scheme to take what belongs to all. The few who dominate the world now, would certainly be pushed aside in favor of freedom for everyone.

Since we can see that this is not the case, at all, one must wonder how such a small group of people can rule over the whole of humanity, and subject them to such a miserable and uneasy existence. The answer is simply because they understand what you don't. They know how to use the natural and psychic powers the Creator has bestowed upon us, so that they may generate a future in which they continue to prosper at your expense. In other words, while your spending all your time and energy worrying about how you can prevent things from happening, they are using their powers, and those that you have ignorantly surrendered, to make sure that certain things do happen.

They know we all have the same power. The power that enables the creation of the physical universe, and the incarnation of living and free willed creatures. We call it the "Generative Principle." Some people have it more than others, or wield it superiorly, take your pick.

This is the power that has allowed you to unfold a micro-universe into the very existence of your own self. An existence that is impossible to deny, because it consists of your own thoughts and your own physical being. Let us call it "Will Power" for right now, or the Will, if you like, either term suits our needs.

If you ask yourself this question. How much do you want something to happen, and how often do you think about it? Then you might realize that the odds are high in favor of the conclusion, that if you really want something, and you think about it a lot, you are going to come up with some ideas about just how you might attain this goal of yours. The better informed you are of what is exactly possible, and what resources you have available to you, the more likely it is that you will succeed in your endeavor.

If the path has already been tread down that road, then the methods and strategies of accomplishing such a goal should be considered as a possible route to your achievement. What obstacles are there? How enthusiastic, or indifferent, are others to your cause? Will they work with you, or against you?

It's true, you are one with the universe, but you are still only one. All share a point of view and have a say in what becomes. When the manifestation of the many becomes possible, they can overwhelm the manifestation of the few. No one, except "The All", can absolve the Cosmos, and impose its will upon the manifestation of reality.

An uneasy feeling has come to grip most of humanity at this point. Even those that know and feel the power of God, may believe themselves to be forsaken at this moment in history. All the hope and promise of almost limitless possibilities, have collapsed into fear and emotional angst. The dream of what we could do with our accumulated knowledge as we pass it on to our offspring, who in turn hand it to their children, has given way to a culture of nihilism. All the dreams and beautiful thoughts, of your own imagination, are swept aside by the cold realities, and the unavoidable consequences, of a creature enslaved to the machinery of a material existence.

If your conception of who you are, or how well you are doing, is based upon your belief of how others see you, then how can you gauge your real success? You do realize it isn't possible to know exactly what someone else is thinking, don't you? Even if they spelled it out for you, in the clearest language that you would understand, could you really be sure that they were telling you the truth? What if they were, and you couldn't reconcile your own thoughts and emotions enough to believe them?

Without a moral compass, and a real knowledge that what you are doing is essential in the creation of a better existence, one cannot achieve happiness. Even a wild animal in the most luxurious of captivities, will become depressed if it does not have to accomplish tasks to survive.

The fact that you may be a struggling artist, just scraping by on your meager earnings, or a multibillionaire, with a mansion and a yacht, will neither, ensure, nor prevent, the happiness and peace of mind that we all seek. The overwhelming factor in the way that you view your own success, is the knowledge of what you have done to achieve your goals. Did you overcome long odds stacked against you, or were you handed the opportunities and luxuries denied to others? Did you participate in arrangements and agreements with others that benefited all, or did you steal and coerce the resources and power you now control? Are you helping people, or are you hurting people?

One of the most beloved and popular of all human social behaviors is participating in gamesmanship. Whether it be competing in actual sporting events, or a pleasant game of checkers, people love to compete, especially against each other. While this is clearly a surrogate for the actual trials and tribulations of our existence, it has blossomed into a replacement for the real concerns and responsibilities of adult life. The very fact that grown men could display the entire spectrum of emotions, from despair, to euphoria, over the fate of a game that they are not even participating in, is a shocking indictment of the modern culture.

Yes, sports and games are a valuable teaching mechanism for children. It affords them to experience the achievement of succeeding in one's goals, while facing genuine opposition, from an opponent whose aims are directly contrary to their own. They learn many important lessons about cooperation and strategies, that prepare them to succeed when they become adults and the outcome of their endeavors is critically important to the wellness of themselves, their families, and the community. The lessons of respect, compassion, and accomplishment, are all conveyed to a person who has participated in friendly competition that people can both win and lose at.

Many people still believe that they can find happiness, and a sense of accomplishment, in a personal association with the success of their favorite sports team, or the material possessions that they see before their eyes. Yet, any objective investigation into the lives of human beings - be they rich, famous, or otherwise - throughout history, will reveal that this is simply not possible. Oh sure, a rich man can be as happy or as miserable as anyone else, but his peace of mind will never come from the gadgets and trinkets, that those without, both, admire, and desire for themselves.

Without the challenges and struggles to create what we so desperately want, there can be no satisfaction in obtaining these things. That is why the love and friendship of a close companion, is always the most treasured of all prizes. For this cannot be fabricated, or bought with any amount of money and/or coercion.

Only the things that cannot be quantifiably measured, and are bestowed upon us freely by others, or gained through accomplishment, truly make us happy. You can only fool yourself for so long, sooner or later you will realize that you still haven't gotten what you really wanted. We certainly need material objects to navigate, and to survive, in this world, but these must be honestly valued for what they are used to do, and for what purpose they serve.

Material is only the stuff we use to create, and the physical universe is the place where we demonstrate our abilities and imagination. This life is short however, but because the powers of creation we possess are superior to the crude matter that manifests as our reality, we can take control of the future.

Clearly, most people have no idea that we are consciously manifesting the physical universe through the power of generation inherent to the mind. Now experimental science has begun to demonstrate that the universe is ultimately a perfectly operating, and very persistent, illusion. The disagreement, and now the only honest philosophical question left to ponder, is whether the universe is an

illusionary concept of the mind, or the mind is an illusionary product of the universe.

Chapter II

The Art of Creating

Most people do understand that they must get up off their tush, and physically do some work, if they want to get something accomplished here. What they don't realize, is that absolutely nothing gets done unless somebody indeed does it. This goes for everything, including the creation of stars and galaxies, the turning of the Earth, and the falling of rain.

Without a prime mover, the law of cause and effect is nullified. Naturally, these things are way above the levels of causation and actualization, that a normal earth creature can understand, or has any influence upon. They also work in a mechanized and predictable fashion. But there is no doubt in the mind of a true believer, that the laws and guiding principles of nature, have been fashioned through the Supreme Will. You can substitute that definition with God, "The All," or the Eternal Consciousness, if you prefer that analogy, but the fact that there is a force that creates, is indisputable.

Before anything can come into existence the thought of it must be entertained. The first principle of Syncromysticism is that all is mind.

Everything you can see, smell, taste, or touch, has been created through the thought process. Everything that exists, has existed, or ever will exist is generated and governed by the infinite powers of the Eternal Consciousness. A materialist obviously disputes this pronouncement, but thousands of humans, have spent hundreds of years, and billions of dollars, trying to figure out just what physical matter is made up of, and they can't find a single piece. Oh sure, they have names for all types, and subcomponents of physical manifestations, but it always boils down to invisible forces and packages of energy. There is nothing inherently solid about a physical object.

If you look at a brick wall, you see an obstacle, but the physicist will assure you that 99.9 percent of that wall is empty space. The same goes for your own body, so they can find no reasonable explanation of why we can't just walk through that wall, other than the fact that we have tried it, and it doesn't work. They do understand, however, that when we collide with this barrier, it is not a collision of matter, but a collision of forces that repels us. The obvious conclusion is that the physical universe is an illusion of consequences.

This illusion is facilitated by the rapid vibration of the medium that we have come to know as matter/energy, and is apparently subject to the powers of the mind. Granted, our individual minds have only a small measure of control, but if we understand the potential uses and purpose of this medium, then we can use our ingenuity and the mechanization of consequences to our own benefit. All life forms do just this in the creation of an organic machine that helps to enhance and direct their powers of generation.

The recognition that all things are in a state of vibration, is a fundamental principle of Syncromysticism. This is not a principle that requires any lengthy discussions for most people to understand, and knowledge of this fact is generally only useful to philosophical and scientific inquiries. The realization of this underlying principle of physical matter has led to the theoretical concept of absolute zero, and to scientific understandings of thermodynamics, and resonance.

Vibration is included in the fundamental principles of Syncromysticism because it applies universally to all generated physical objects, and provides insight into the operations of this persistent illusion. It makes it clear to all, that potential energy is contained within the physical objects that constitute the known universe.

Taking advantage of potential energy is an extremely useful tactic towards your own success in any endeavor. Anyone who has ever felt the rushing tide of water, or sailed upon the windswept sea, will understand what I'm talking about. The powers of "The All," and the functions of the universe, cannot be overcome by beings that wield an infinitesimal fraction of the Generative Principle. We can, however, work in harmony with the forces that both surround us, and bind us together, in the creation of future realities that suit our own desires.

This concept of working in conjunction with superior forces leads into another important principle of Syncromysticism, the principle of

Correspondence. This is the understanding of how the universe operates on a common conceptual theme throughout all levels of manifestation.

Even though they may be separated by chasms in the plains of existence, essential elements of physical manifestation are shared universally. We allude to this in the micro-verse description of a human being. Though it may be true that you have no idea of how your body effectively functions, there is no doubt that you are in control of all these operations, even if only subconsciously.

Materialists love to talk about enzymes, and proteins, engaged in chemical reactions and working in a mechanized fashion, when they attempt to explain the mysteries of life. They always gloss over the fact, that every organism, and all the enzymes, proteins, and divergent cellular structures in a living organism, are constructed by a single cell, from scratch.

You may have wondered how the cells in your body understand what their primary functions are, or how they perceive anything at all without sense organs. Considering that you cannot read something without knowing what the symbols used to convey a language mean. How is it possible that a single cell can decipher an informational system, and implement a transformation of its own physical existence, without access to the powers of the mind? It can even unleash abilities totally alien to its own species through the introduction of foreign DNA.

In fact, the ability to develop independently into the specific types of cells that are required to construct and operate a human body, rules out the theory of mechanized chemical reaction. You cannot argue that the act of reproduction is the result of unintended circumstances and the proximity of chemical compounds, because organic cells are not just replicating themselves, they are clearly varying their design.

Although the DNA in the nucleus of the cells is identical, and indeed the zygote at first divides into exact replications of its original composition. Ultimately, each individual cell must embark on its own unique course of action. How is any cell supposed to realize what course of generation it must follow, without access to the feedback of perspective? Do you know what a single cell perceives as its own self image? We of course view it as a little sphere of chemical compounds, and the materialist doesn't believe a single cell possesses the powers of the mind at all, but again, if it didn't, how could it understand the information contained within the DNA, and generate anything at all?

The principle of Correspondence is the component that puts the synchronicity in the mysticism. The mystical part being the powers of the mind. Without the principle of Correspondence, it would not be possible for all conscious beings to have access to the universal mind. Synchronicity is manifested throughout all the plains of conscious existence. The implementation of this structural necessity, enables the omnipotence of "The All" over the generation of the Cosmos. Like "The All," you are essentially the deity of your own micro-universe.

The mystic understands that the universe is a thought experiment. As a human being you find yourself on a very high plain of conscious awareness. Just how high up we are, there is no way of knowing, because the levels of consciousness are truly infinite. We are aware enough to inquire into the generation of the cosmos, and to apply the forces of nature in the development and command of technology, so there is no doubt that we are at an advanced stage.

We now possess the ability to overcome the natural obstacles of our ascendancy to the supreme position in the determination of planetary consequences. In other words, we can now take control of the physical manifestation of reality, through a point of view that originates inside the phenomena. This can be either, extremely beneficial, or extremely dangerous, to the continuation of our existence.

The powers of the mind, and the forces of nature originate externally of the physical world, and so are not beholden to such a limited perspective. When the Christian Messiah stated that none are without sin, He was speaking about the contamination of the mind that occurs through its union with a physical incarnation. Exercising dominance over the manifestations of future realities by obviously limited intelligence, can only compare to having complete control of your own dream.

We all have dreams, not the desires and wants of this world, but the ones that we have in our sleep. Sometimes the ability to discern if what is taking place is really happening, or is taking place only in our own mind, can be tough to do. I normally don't remember my dreams, but there are plenty of times that I do. When you dream, do you have any conscious measure of control over what is being generated for you to see? How do you see something with your eyes closed and your face jammed in a pillow, anyway?

In the dreams that I remember, I often question what they mean, or if they mean anything at all. This is quite an ancient and widespread human behavior, so I don't give it too much thought. Instead I seem to fixate upon why I couldn't do the things that I wanted to do, at the time that the opportunities to do them, arose in the dream. Is that odd? Perhaps you have experienced these thoughts as well.

Here in the physical universe we exist as human beings fully aware of the operating forces that govern the known universe. With this knowledge, and with the tools that we possess, we are in position to accomplish anything. Though not exactly everything is possible, technically, anything is possible. You just need to broaden the scope and theme of the concept.

I will go on the record right now, and state that it is not possible to undo what has already been done. Nor is it possible to progress to a specific point without undergoing the actions of causation. Thus, the idea of "time travelling" is specifically untenable. You can, however, learn from experience and determine the resulting outcome of reality. You may also make amends, and so even though the reality of what has previously occurred cannot be removed from actuality, the situation can often be rectified, and that's what really counts.

The Generative Principle is what allows us to carry on this thought experiment. Just like the treading of rushing water, however, or the navigation of space and seas, we cannot use its power to overcome the principles of Correspondence, or the will of universal consciousness. It must be used with an understanding of the laws of cause and effect, and will manifest as a physical reality that cannot be undone. Yes, the brutal master we humans call time is a major component of the Generative Principle. It is the prime indicator of the unfolding of reality through the mechanism and principle of "Cause and Effect."

By using the motions of physical properties as a measuring device, we are capable of, revealing the past, and anticipating the future. For us everything that manifests, does so now. We are always living in the now. We can envision the future, and remember the past, but you are experiencing something that is happening right now.

To generate the future that you want to experience, you must understand what is currently happening. If you falsely believe that something is occurring that really isn't, or vice versa, then your efforts to generate a desired outcome to the situation are greatly reduced. It still may be possible, but in a world where competing visions of the future manifest as a shared reality, knowledge is power.

The human species has developed the capacity to wield extraordinary power over our planet. We can anticipate the motions of our world, and manipulate the forces of nature with technology. This power, of course, brings with it the possibilities of abuse, which is exactly what we have quickly done with it. The desire to control all aspects of the developing world that we inhabit, is destroying the human ecosystem, along with a whole lot of other species as well.

The question to ask here is, why is this reality being generated, instead of a much happier one, that the overwhelming majority of people, all over the world, desire for themselves, their families, and their friends? Where is the peace on Earth, and the good will towards men? Well, there are only really two possible answers, and it may in fact be a combination of both. Either, the people of the world don't have the slightest idea about how to generate a reality in which we can live in peace, and without major discord, or people deliberately seek to destroy other human beings, and to exploit them for their own selfish benefit.

I happen to believe that both these things are true, and it has more than just a little bit to do with our current situation. The problem I have with this conclusion, is that the people who say they want peace and prosperity for all, far outweigh the people who are benefiting from the exploitation of humanity and the planet. This means there are billions of clueless souls walking the face of the Earth, without the slightest idea that they are primarily responsible for the problem.

I know that people do have knowledge of living with each other in a generally peaceful manner, and have previously existed harmoniously with other cultures and species. How then can they just sit back and watch only a few benefit from the absolute exploitation of so many?

Obviously, the answer is ignorance, but it's not an ignorance of facts, it's an ignorance of truth. The overwhelming majority of people are so out of touch with what is really occurring to them, that they believe they must pay other people to live in an environment which they were born into.

I mean think about it, I'm not saying you can't exchange goods and services with other people. If you want someone to do something for you, and they say "ok, I'll do that for this," then there is no problem. The problem is, that people have come to believe, that an institution which threatens them with physical harm, if they do not turn money over to it and obey its bureaucratic dictates, is bringing peace and harmony to the community in which they reside. How can you not recognize that this is absurd?

It can only be, because of their ignorance. They ignore the truth of what is right and wrong, and we ignore the misdeeds of humanity out of fear of reprisals. This fear is of course the weapon of your masters, always lauded over us, so that we act in a familiar manner. You instinctively act in predictable ways that they can both anticipate and understand.

Our behavior and decision making is so dependent upon the avoidance of negative perceptions and consequences, that it can only be classified as reactionary. This is how the elite plan and generate the future of humanity. A future that always leaves them in control of the state, the church, the media, and of course solidifying that power through the current incarnation of the monetary system, which at this point is a complete monopoly.

For us though, if we understand these truths, then we can walk the system back to our own advantage. Revolutions of all types come and go, change is the only constant in the universe. To believe that the present situation cannot be resolved in our favor is pure nonsense. It is going to take a lot more of us to get on board with what needs to be done, though, and the first step down that path, is awareness. Once this reaches critical mass, we can set a course of action on how to deal with the problem. This is, of course, standard operation problem solving, and doesn't necessarily involve any mystical powers or herculean efforts. We do, however, need to realize that the mystical powers, we do possess, have been turned against us, and now work on behalf of the elitists.

It will also require the people of the world to pay more attention to the most pressing and pertinent issues of societal conflict, instead of who won the game, or who is sleeping with whom. We must use our own time and energy to throw off the spell of our overlords, and see the world for what it is, because, unless we break free from the conditions of fear and ignorance that dominates our understanding of the world, we can never understand just how warped our society has become.

The synchronistic angle requires us to work in concert with Natural Law, to be sure that people are not being wrongly penalized by the revolution, and that their unalienable rights are not trampled by the mass hysteria that the ruling class will surely instigate.

Employing the powers of mystical correspondence does not mean we all just need to think positively, and push out those negative thoughts, or accept any of that other hokey new age bullshit, that today's morally bankrupt society loves to indulge themselves in. Just thinking about something or wishing for results isn't going to make that reality materialize. Yes, we need to visualize the future we hope to create, but you must envision all the possibilities that might come to fruition when you are planning a course of action, then act upon, and in favor of, your desired goals. Both the good, and the bad things, must be considered, if you are to plan well and execute properly.

A condition of mindfulness serves us, by prompting subconscious, and timely actions, that help direct the physical principles of cause and effect. Only these tactics can ultimately produce a successful outcome for our endeavors. Any other course will result in the failure of humanity to advance beyond the realm of a purely animalistic existence.

Chapter III

The Laws of Attraction

Many people have a general idea of what Karma is, and try to incorporate it into their own brand of spirituality. The laws of attraction are represented throughout the plains of existence, both spiritually, and physically, and most people are bound to run across their manifestations at certain points in the moments of their lives. Just trying to be a good person isn't enough, however, because there are, of course, those who will prey on the kindness of others and take advantage to the detriment of the unsuspecting victim.

It takes more than just goodwill, to create a future that is both, beneficial to ourselves, and protects us from oppression and tyranny. It takes a vigilant commitment to morality, and the performance of righteous behavior towards all aspects of social interaction.

So yes, Karma and the Golden Rule, are tenets of Syncromysticism, but they are only simplistic summations of the cosmic consequences, that arise due to the inherent dualism of universal manifestation. This dualism is displayed within most of the principles of mysticism, the exception being, of course, the recognition of "The All."

The principles of both Polarity, and Gender, bring the inherent dualism of the Cosmos front and center to those whom seek to perceive reality. Let us examine a concept that most people claim to have an opinion on, and knowledge of, and that subject is, specifically, the difference between what is right and what is wrong.

Without an understanding of what is right, and what is wrong, one is not able to discern if their actions fall in line with their own version of Karmic justice, or the Golden Rule. Without this knowledge, there would be no basis for the rule of law, or any possibility of obtaining justice through retribution.

Since all these things are taking place, you would think that most people understand the difference between right and wrong, and if you ask them about it, they will tell you that they indeed do. Do they really? Where, and how, did they learn the difference? Do their ideas about the subject conflict? Are they sure about their convictions, if so, how sure?

If you think that you understand the difference between right and wrong, simply because it's written down in some religious text, or is instituted into a societies legal system, then I assure you, that our efforts at achieving a desirable future civilization will most certainly fail.

An examination of available human history can be referenced for confirmation if you wish. Right and wrong, or good an evil, are just different aspects of the same concept which we have come to call judgment. The duality of the Cosmos is both, a correspondent feature found on all the plains of existence, and displayed most notably in Syncromysticism by the principle of Polarity.

Polarity is somewhat akin to the concept of opposites. We understand big and small as different, only because they are polarities of size. There is no permanent characteristic or difference in description of an object necessary for us to consider that object big, or small. These terms are only used in comparative instances, so that we may describe the size of the subject in relation to another object.

The fact that a specific object need not change in anyway, at all, and we can describe its size along a spectrum of extremities that can be described as infinite, displays the importance of the principle of Polarity to any comparative situation. In a universe that is founded with the concept of duality inherent in the physical design, Polarity is the most obvious expression of this duality in the actual manifestation of objects and concepts.

The principle of Gender is more about recognizing the separation of an entirety. It is the duality that negates itself in an act of unification when the two parts come together. Often the creative energies and forces of the Universe exist in a state of separation. When they at last come together, the fusion of the two partners often results in a new medium, or the generation of kinetic physical actions.

The better examples of this principle, are the comparisons of male and female, or positive and negative. With the synthesis of these two essential components, exciting results are manifested in a specific, and timely executed combination of properties.

It's important to understand that these are concepts and principles of action. There are no authoritarian writings, or councils to enforce the teachings of the faith. Most of these principles have been handed down through any number of long gone ancient cults, over thousands of years. None of these ideas are modern in anyway, but they are all supported by the most current scientific evidence.

I have not seen or heard of one religious doctrine or dogma, that does not contain blatantly false ideology. Which is why Syncromysticism doesn't really contain any specific ideology. It is more of a recognition of the situation that exists, and a methodology that helps to produce a more desirable future for its practitioners. It doesn't contain the type of rhetoric and dogma that has been used to foment wars, sow division, and exploit humanity.

Yes, there are some good philosophical and theological ideas in all religions, and usually one self-evident truth, that is at the core of all of them. Mostly it is this one inherent truth that brings the people to the pulpit. They all also contain any number of superstitious, and/or meaningless practices and rituals too. So only those, who can discern the difference between the two, can successfully incorporate their beliefs into a functioning society, and a successful personal experience.

The modern equivalent of this false religion is pseudo-environmentalism. There is a core truth behind the understanding, that humanity has a measurable and reciprocal influence upon the environment we use to generate our future. There are also people whom care about this enlightening knowledge, and they now desire to actively focus upon it. These people have decided to directly affect the outcome of the accumulated consequences of cause and effect.

Exercising the Generative Principle, they now attempt to control the feedback of the inherent structure of "Cause and Effect." This interplay is then expressed through the principle of Rhythm. The oscillation of instance, between cause, and effect, produces the rhythm that your mind uses to perceive progress. This progression of the current situation is known to human beings as time.

A conceptual measurement that arises from the perceptions of the conscious mind, "Time" is strictly a categorizing principle of observation. The conscious and sentient properties, that are designated as the powers of mind, do not require time to perform their own inherent operations.

Time is strictly a property of physical reality. As such a thing, it can only be quantified in the terms of physical actions. In one word, time is change, but it is a change that requires motion be included in its definition. Likewise, change can only be described as a function of time, because its measurement is the very definition of time.

If nothing in the universe changed, not one molecular vibration has occurred, nor one atomic oscillation, nor quantum leap or shift, has taken place between any specific particle, and/or its relation to any other, then no time has passed. This is what we call "the moment," a moment in time.

The powers of the mind are not bound by time. The mind sees things as they are, how they were, and for what they can still be, simultaneously. It doesn't require any physical components at all, and it can envision the entirety of the changes that will result from the very motions that it has previously witnessed. It transcends the limitations of the principles that create the physical universe, and that manifest themselves in an eternal chain of cause and effect. A manifestation that is both responsible, and essential, in the generation of a definable event.

Outside the boundaries of cause and effect, the mind is free to generate its desired future, by interfering in the anticipated course of causation. As it does this, it also recognizes the consequences that have arisen from its actions. The principle of Rhythm is thus the manifestation of the power of free will that is exercised by a choice to alter the path of the generating future.

Thus, the laws of attraction are only attempts to describe the connection between two facets of the corresponding features of our reality. Of course, there are consequences to the choices you make, if there were none, then you haven't really made a choice. To make a choice, one must be able to define a difference in the outcomes of their decisions. The principle of Polarity allows us to simplify the perception of that outcome, with the minimum required characteristics of a defined concept. Is it better or worse? Are there more, or less?

If you recognize that the choices you are making are leading towards the future you describe as negative, then you will define those choices as bad choices. The principle of Polarity allows us to extend the severity of the concept of judgement. We can now use this principle to categorize this judgement to the extreme. Thus, the choices you made can be described as extremely bad, which is, as humans say, evil. One can now ascribe a mystical definition to the recognition of a fundamental truth. The recognition of this truth in the eastern religions is called Karma. It is only a quantification of the consequences that arise, from the principles of Syncromysticism, both generating, and manifesting, as the future.

The principle of Gender encompasses the definition of categorizing a distinct difference, into a defining characteristic. It is a principle that we can use to minimize the quantification of any concept, so that we may incorporate it into a wider conceptualization.

The principle of Gender is not related to the laws of attraction in the same way that Rhythm and Polarity are. It need not be present in the manifestation of a physical object, or a generated outcome. It is not fundamental to the display of duality that is presented in the generation of physical reality the way Polarity is. Rather, it is the principle that is displayed when we distinctly separate the fundamental properties of a given concept.

The essential difference of whether something is bound by the principle of Polarity, or the principle of Gender, is the distinction between the concept being subject to a description that can include any of the conceptual properties, or if a description of that thing must exclude some characteristics or features that encompass a specific concept. When one engages in categorizing something as big or small, or hot and cold, then this is a quantification of Polarity, as the opposite description may also be applicable to the subject. When one quantifies something as male or female, or as positive or negative, then one is applying the principle of Gender to that concept, because the opposing qualification cannot be applied in a description of the subject.

The laws of attraction are indeed a reflection of the inherent dualism of the physical universe. In our attempt to isolate a specific property of any universal manifestation, we must apply one of these principles to the subject, so that we may limit the concept and impose a specific quality on it. This quality is forever linked by the dualistic nature of all things that exist in our universe, and so we can gain insight into any concept or action by applying the correct principle of inherent dualism to that thing.

If something is small, then that thing is only small, because what we have compared it to, is big. If something is incomplete, or devoid of a specific trait that is necessary to define a complete concept, it is because the separation of these properties serves to isolate and delay the manifestation of effect that is generated by the cause of bringing these parts together.

Chapter IV

The Tenants of Natural Law

Now would be the time to ask how the tenants and philosophies of Syncromysticism could possibly be any better than traditional religious sects. Well perhaps they are not, that is for you to decide, because for any mystical efforts to succeed, one must believe, totally, in the process of mind above matter. That is why we prefer to think of our practices and theological philosophies as guiding principles, and not as specific commandments that must be obeyed. The behavior that you employ, and the moral principles that guide your decisions, are the dominating factor in what type of future your effort generates, but you must really know that your actions are favored by the Divine Spirit, and thus will enhance the probability of your success. We have ethical principles also, and I will try to explain the overriding moral codes of Syncromysticism with a simple explanation of Natural Law.

I didn't get into exactly what Karma is, because it's a Buddhist principle. An eastern understanding of Natural Law and inherent dualism, that incorporates reincarnation into the laws of attraction. I don't want to go beyond the realm of the world that we are presently immersed within, because I understand that the results of both moral, and amoral behavior, are expressly manifested onto our physical plain of existence. As the proverbial saying states, "You reap what you sow."

Transcendental consequences of earthly behavior must always remain speculation. If one proclaims that the results of human adherence to Natural Law are observable and definable on this plain of existence, then it is incumbent on them to appropriately demonstrate this principle. We must always define our success with honest and measurable results, the ones we can quantify with the joy and admiration we experience in our own lives.

The art of Syncromysticism does incorporate many different axioms into its core principles, and makes no bones about where they originated, or who espouses them. It's kind of like Jeet Kune Do, which is the martial arts style developed and taught by Master Bruce Lee. We take what is known to work, and use it in the situations where it can be applied successfully.

Natural Law is the understanding of the principles that bring forth the success of a communal organization, and protects the rights of the individuals bestowed upon them by the Creator. In America, we spell this out in the Declaration of Independence, and further elaborate upon it in the Bill of Rights. Unfortunately, thanks to the indoctrination of our citizenry through the abysmal public school system, most people have no idea that our government is supposed to exist to ensure these rights, not circumvent them through complex legislation and the neglect of an ignorant public. They have almost gotten to the point where they can convince the people that somehow the constitution is outdated, and should be abolished.

Not that they need to do that, because just about every law on the books today is in violation of this important document, and the American people are just not smart enough to realize it. They believe in the system, regardless of how corrupt it has become, and how much oppression they face because of it. They confuse order with freedom, and politicians with leaders, all to the detriment of our own country and to the horror of the nations we conquer and loot.

The people of other nations have the same problems. There are troubles and looming disasters threatening all the peoples and nations of the world. They don't understand Natural Law any better than modern Americans do, in fact, I would argue that a squirrel has a better understanding of the rights bestowed upon it by the Creator.

Most people believe that the rest of the species on this planet live by the law of the jungle. They then like to conveniently narrow that concept down to a typical oversimplification, such as, kill or be killed, or survival of the fittest. Careful examination of the lives and habits of earth creatures in comparison to humanity demonstrates just how wrong these ideas are.

The natural threats to human beings on this planet are the same as they are for all species, weather, predators, disease, and the availability of food sources. Only human beings subjugate their own species so that a few of us may benefit, by the efforts, and at the expense, of the rest of us.

We call this progress because we possess material constructs that have never existed before, that is, if you believe the historians. Other arguments can be made for life expectancy or scientific knowledge, but do these things really make our lives better than a bear, or a bird?

If you examine the present state of human affairs, I doubt that one could argue that humanity lives better than nearly any other species. Surely some people live better than others, but when the quality of life for the entire species is weighed, human life can be described as brutish, nasty, and short. As for science and technology, it has brought us just as much, if not more, trouble, than it has alleviated. It should be clear to all that we are doing something wrong. What are we doing wrong? We are breaking Natural Law. Thus, the laws of attraction, or Karma if you like, is generating a future that balances the equation.

There are generally only three laws that human beings need to follow to produce a society that benefits all of humanity. Don't assault other people, don't steal the stuff that they produce, and don't trespass into their private lairs. It's basically that simple. It is pretty much the same way the other Earth species live, so it's should be clear to all that it works. Most people also don't have a problem adhering to these general principles, so why they cannot be respected is quite perplexing to most.

Why is it that these types of violations occur regularly among human beings, if they overwhelmingly profess a desire to live and let live? Quite simply, it is the very system of human laws and customs, that is producing the mass suffering and dissatisfaction among the people of the world.

Human greed, and lust for power, are responsible for the current ways in which we organize our societies, and because these systems are founded upon the principles of theft and assault, they produce negative feedback that permeates every facet of daily life. Of course, people want to deny this, but the fact is, that the law is guilty of the very things that it was enacted to prevent. How is it that a colony of insects can foster its own prosperity without laws and authorities, but it is implied that humans could never do this? Are we not as evolved as a colony of ants?

As the dominant species on the planet, with all the tools we possess and the knowledge passed on from generations uncountable, we should be able to produce the utopian paradise that we all would love to inhabit. I am sure that it is possible, and even the most cynical social commentator would have to agree, even if they don't believe that it is likely. The reason it isn't being accomplished, is because the methods the public supports to accomplish this task are not suitable for just such a thing. The proof is in the results.

Now there is a small group of very wealthy and powerful people who benefit from the current system, and would like it to remain as it is, you may have heard this referred to as the "status quo." They understand the Generative Principle, and they know that you must want the social institutions, and the governance of human authority, to exist, for them to come into being. If the people didn't want these things, and refused to participate in the construction and operation of them, they would not be here. People foolishly believe that these institutions and agencies exist to serve them, so we demand that they exist, and support them.

Meanwhile they keep funneling more and more of the wealth and resources of humanity to the few people at the top of the pyramid. This is what they are indeed designed to do, whether you know it or not. Your human masters get you to help them generate the mechanism that ensures their own wealth and power, because you believe that these mechanisms promote your safety and well being.

Yes, it's a complicated and obfuscated system. It started way back with the invention of royalty, and continues to persist today as a technocracy, but the result is still the same. Of course, you were born into this world when the system was already advanced to the point of near perfection, and that's part of the reason it all seems so normal to you. Under close examination however, it is nothing but the modern incarnation of slavery. Yes, it is a kinder gentler form of slavery, but it is slavery none the less.

The great prince Siddhartha, now known as Buddha to the world, famously stated that, "If God does not prevent evil, he is not good, and if God cannot prevent evil, then he is not God." This may seem like a pretty harsh statement, especially coming from one who is revered as a religious icon by billions of people around the world, but it requires us to examine it fully before we accept or condemn it. What exactly did he mean? What kind of God was he talking about?

I believe Siddhartha was trying to get across the idea, that the evils and suffering that humanity endures are not the result of God's will, but the result of humans who simply don't recognize that it is our own actions, and failure to live correctly, that result in the manifestation of human misery on Earth.

He preached that this misery could surely be abated with the performance of "right action," by both individuals, and the institutions they create. He was, in effect, stating that the Divine Spirit punishes humanity for its amoral behavior. We certainly can live a life of peaceful and rewarding experiences, but the most important gift of free will, requires a corrective mechanism, to enlighten those who choose to live wrongly. One that allows for the experience and development of individual and autonomous spiritual growth. If we break the rules we suffer the consequences. This is the lesson we must learn and accept, on our own, and for ourselves. For if the Divine Spirit ensures the perfection of existence through its own omnipotence, then it has created nothing at all.

You would think that this is an easy enough concept to understand, yet most of humanity has tremendous difficulty in understanding who makes the rules, and exactly what they are. Their ignorance of what the Creator really is, and their desire to define God as an anthropomorphic super being, has limited their own ability to see the truth, and to benefit from the powers that the Creator has bestowed upon them.

The mystic understands that the universe is governed by the Supreme Will. If you follow God's rules, which are the natural laws that I previously laid out, and that no one seems to have a problem with, the results of human endeavors will result in a peaceful and prosperous community.

Those who believe it's necessary to have millions of legislated rules and regulations, all enforced with the use of violence and confiscation, are the ones enabling the human misery and suffering that exists within the world. If you follow man's laws, instead of Natural Law, then the result is clearly observable, and demonstrated by the world we have come to know.

Now it certainly is a part of human nature to petition the Gods for favor. These traditions go way back, and take the form of many types of ritualistic human behaviors. These include prayer, sacrifice, fasting, and even the superstitious behaviors of wood knocking or crossing your fingers. Most humans already accept the idea of obtaining favorable assistance from otherwise invisible and undetectable forces. Why would anyone doubt me if I told them it was true?

Most likely what they would dispute is the method by which you can attain the assistance of these cosmic forces, whatever you may believe they are. Usually people have already been given their own religious preferences through the observed behavior of family and community, but people do change their minds about things. For whatever reason,

someone decides to abandon their current ideas or beliefs, they often use that same reason to replace them with a new set.

People convert from one religion to another, or give up on their beliefs entirely, all the time. I can't say what they are looking for, exactly, or if they will ever find it. Whatever makes you happy is as potent a force for personal improvement as any religion or philosophy can be. If you are not hurting anybody else, who can say you are wrong?

If an individual philosophy or mindset happens to be an original concept, or has borrowed from the conclusions that other humans may have reached over the eons of human history, is irrelevant to the person who adopts these beliefs. Of course, the organized religions want to demand that you accept and conform to the beliefs that constitute their own brand of piety. This gives them greater control and insight into the way their followers will think and behave, which is of course all the better for controlling valuable human resources.

The syncromysticist is an independent thinker. We are not opposed to working with others towards common causes, or embracing the teachings of any prophet or sage, if they concur with the realizations that we have arrived at. Our decisions and actions are our own, and we take complete ownership and full accountability for the outcomes they produce.

Each, and every individual, is contributing to the manifestation of our world, and helping to determine the end results of human civilization. Your input matters, and is necessary for the progress that future generations will work with, and build upon. Unfortunately, most people have outsourced their creative contributions to organizations and institutions, so these entities have become very powerful actors in determining the outcome of future events. Your role pretty much consists of turning over an increasing share of what you produce, to these engines of creation and the people who control them. You are also giving up a lot of your own ability to determine your everyday affairs, because you have become dependent upon a system that treats you as a cog in the machinery of its global corporate empire.

The only way out is to get in touch with the Generative Principle, and to recognize what it's going to take to create a better future. This can be done on an individual basis, but there are billions of directed peoples all over the world, visualizing a common idea of what the future is going to look like, and what steps must be taken to get there. A powerful and pervasive mass perception that is continually opposing your individual dreams. This is the cumulative psychosis of a popular culture, that an elite group of movers and shakers feeds into the minds of the public, through their stranglehold on the mass media, the arts, and the entertainment industries. All with the help of well trained and highly paid psychologists, and learned practitioners of the neurosciences, who specialize in human behavioral norms.

The system is so completely pervasive, that to try and escape its absolute grip on everything you have come to depend upon is utterly futile. You cannot work outside the matrix of lies, and still effectively function as an agent of alternative generation. What we need, is an infiltration of the institutions that control the information and direct public policy.

We cannot simply destroy a device that is used to facilitate the advancement of human interaction, without having another method or mechanism in place to continue our progressions. The system must be retaken by the users and re-orientated to serve our own many viewpoints instead of the world domination desired by the power brokers running the game.

Chapter V

Christ Consciousness

A lot of people are willing to try almost anything, to recognize some type of fulfillment in their lives, or get in touch with God, whatever their vision of the Deity may be. Millions swear they have been "saved" by, or "found" Jesus, yet, they continue to support institutions, and facilitate the oppression of the people, by the same "legal" processes that murdered their beloved savior.

The laws of man must be recognized as imperfect, and understood to be insufficient to ensure that true justice is conveyed to the people they claim to serve. Only when you finally realize this, can you begin to understand the truth behind Natural Law, and apply the principles discussed here, to the decisions you make while navigating this world. This is the art of Syncromysticism.

If one truly wishes to follow Christ, then one must act in the way that Christ demonstrated by his own moral actions, and then live with the consequences that they produce. One should not hesitate to give up their earthly existence, if it is done so standing up for the moral principles that God has bestowed upon all creatures.

If you realize that all is mind, then you recognize that only the physical incarnation is destroyed when death is generated through righteous actions. The spirit of moral action continues to manifest upon creation, and the righteous cause that you have sacrificed your life in favor of, continues to fill the conscious thoughts of those who are left behind to generate the coming future. Believers know the Divine Spirit favors the thoughts and concepts that create the beauty and harmony it desires, while dismissing those it finds abhorrent or nonproductive.

The syncromysticist understands that a physical re-manifestation of Jesus Christ is not going to take place. We prefer to emulate the behavior of the Christian savior by acting in accord with "Christ Consciousness." This we define as the ability to balance both our thoughts, and our emotions, so that we may make the right choices, and take the right actions, in any situation, no matter how difficult or stressful the circumstances. We know it is the people of this earth whom have allowed the lies of the statist, and the evils of institutional authority, to plague mankind and diminish the existence of humanity.

Just how one may participate in "Christ Consciousness" needs to be explained before we move any further into understanding the Generative Principle. We all have the ability and continue to generate the future events that arise through the principle of "Cause and Effect." As we currently live in an "information" age, anyone alive today knows, credible information is the key to understanding and recognizing any situation at all. The most important aspect of obtaining "Christ

Consciousness" is that you know actual truth. I'm not talking about "facts", although they are certainly helpful. When we speak of "Truth" we are talking about universalism, things that matter in any situation, all the time.

The principles that I have discussed here are manifested throughout the entire universe on all plains of existence, and at every level of consciousness. Living in an age of technological achievement, we have even discovered a way to engineer results at the atomic level. This understanding of the enormous amount of energy that is contained within the smallest manifestations of physical reality, has inspired humanity to try and unlock this energy for our own use. The people who have done this were obviously very intelligent people. They understood the "facts" of atomic structures and theory, as discovered and demonstrated by the scientists who came before them, and who's contributions they built upon.

What they didn't consider was Truth. The truth about human nature, the truth of the repercussions of cause and effect, or the truth about what type of energy is destructive vs. creative, and the corresponding synchronization that comes with the unleashing of such a destructive force. Now we stand on the brink of worldwide annihilation, as the future we rush toward reflects the destructive power that we have generated. The proliferation of nuclear weapons and deadly radioactive waste threatens countless species, including our own. All because they never really thought about the effects of using universal forces to accomplish the feats of murder, conquest and intimidation.

You may well have figured out that we cannot always succeed in generating the future result we desired to achieve. Of course, there are many possible reasons why the actual results of any situation have come to pass, or failed to materialize. The important thing to realize is that you have mindful influence over the events that occur in your life, but by no means do you have complete control.

Proponents of using nuclear energy will make any argument, valid or not, to try and convince humanity that it is beneficial for us. In some instances, it most certainly is, such is the nature of a universe that has the principles of duality incorporated into its existence. In actual practice, though, the use of this type of destructive energy has negative consequences that far outweigh its positive influences on the existence of humanity. It's use and development are not immune from the laws of causation, and have manifested under the law of unintended consequences. Which is just a fancy name for admitting that you either, didn't think things completely through, or you just don't know what the hell you're messing with.

This influence you have on the unfolding of the universe is real, and the most obvious way you demonstrate and impress your desires upon the world is through your actions. This is the clear and concrete evidence that the thoughts we have, are the beginnings of the reality that will manifest as our very lives, and that once you act upon your desires, the resulting outcome is externalized as physical reality. A manifestation that is now subject to all universal laws and principles. Only actions undertaken with mindful consciousness, benefit from the mystic powers of Correspondence, and produce a favorable outcome. One that does not generate pain and suffering, but instead love and satisfaction.

The realization that your actions are not born only from your thoughts, but require some level of reflection about how they will make you feel once implemented, is an important development in the maintenance of your mental health.

Like all things that are generated in the universe, the synchronicity of Correspondence requires the duality of the cosmos to be expressed in your consciousness. Our actions arise out of the synthesis of our thoughts and our emotions, so giving too much weight to one or the other leads to an imbalance in our psyche, and our lives. A proper combination of thoughtful action results in the exaltation of freewill and gives birth to the concept of morality.

Neuroscience likes to quantify the duality of consciousness in a purely materialistic manner. They will talk about the left brain / right brain aspects or characteristics of human consciousness, because they believe that cognizance originates from the brain.

The mystic understands that sentience is only manifested through the brain, if the incarnated creature is fortunate enough to have one. You, must also come to understand that consciousness is the ultimate source and origin of all things, and that, you yourself, can only be quantified as something that thinks. What this thinking thing is defined as, varies from culture to culture, but for this topic we will identify it as the Spirit.

The Spirit is divine, and as such, its union with the flesh mimics the duality of the generated Cosmos. The infinite division of the Divine Spirit is what has introduced the principle of Gender into the Cosmos. This duality is most easily understood in terms that are instinctually apparent to human beings, and so have come to be known as the divine feminine aspect, and the divine male aspect of the Spirit.

The correspondence with the physical science would be that the right/brain aspects relate to the emotional and introspective components of the psyche, and the left/brain aspects are represented by the impulsive and definitive components. Mystics identify the creative aspects of our consciousness as a feminine characteristic, categorizing the drive to perform the action, and the determination to produce the desired result as a male trait.

Of course, all humans share both these traits and either one can be dominant in males or females. The proper balance of both these characteristics is what makes a well balanced and intelligent person. One could never attain "Christ Consciousness," though, without a working knowledge of universal truth, and an understanding of the difference between right and wrong. Unfortunately, no one is going to teach them this, because then people would begin to understand the illegitimacy of their own subjugation. That is why the academic institutions prefer to teach moral relativism, which I see as completely amoral, because when you consider that if morality can be relative, then you really don't have any morals at all.

Overly emotional, or impulsive people can find it extremely difficult to achieve the results that they desire to see become a reality. They are also easily manipulated by those who understand behavioral norms and patterns. The world is filled with both appeals to your emotions, and encouragements to act on your impulses. All the time imploring you to take actions that may satiate your immediate desires, but in fact, are just a call to act on behalf of those who truly benefit by your actions. They don't really care why you did it, just do it.

You must understand that regardless of your point of view, or how you want to define the ability of a conscious individual to act, all actions originated in thought. That which controls your thoughts, controls your actions. Since you can only be defined as a thinking thing, whatever has control of your thoughts, does indeed have control of you. A battle ensues, between Spirit, and Soul, and you must once again reconcile the inherent dualism that corresponds to the nature of a union between creator and creation.

The emotions that arise out of love or fear, tend to try and regulate your actions before you take them. That is why direct appeals to these regulating aspects of consciousness are extremely successful in subliminally spurring you into action. In what amounts to no actual time at all, you have initiated action that was predetermined to be immediately beneficial to you, regardless of the fact, that you understand the consequences of the action may be detrimental to the achievement of the goals you are working towards.

Reflex actions, and instinctual behavior, are believed by most, to be actions that are taken without thought, the mystic knows this is pure rubbish. EVERYTHING has arisen out of thought. The materialist will not dispute that your thoughts can be controlled, and sorcerers, magicians, psychologists, neuro-engineers and just plain con-men, are forever seeking to do just this. Therefore, to argue that by controlling your thoughts, they can control your actions, even they must admit, that subconscious and reactive actions originate through the thought process.

Understanding that the duality of consciousness is felt by you, as both, the desire to act, (your will) and as a reason to act, (your emotions) will only help you to reach your intended goals and manifest in the satisfaction of achievement.

If one practiced moral habits, and only acted beneficially towards those whom he shares his world with, then that person has reached an enlightened state of mind. He or She has achieved "Christ Consciousness." Emotions don't rule, impulses don't control actions, and morality is given noted preference. Thus, the actions that are taken result in a preferable future outcome to all concerned.

One may ask how the outcome of being crucified was a preferable outcome for the Christian savior, and if you ask this question to the theologians, you would receive any number of disparities for an answer. No Christian would ever argue that the outcome of his actions were not the most important ones ever taken by a human being. He wouldn't be viewed as a "savior" if his actions were not heroic and sparing of lives.

Regardless of your religious affiliations, or beliefs, the value systems and liberal humanistic attitudes of even atheists, is rooted in the spiritual teachings of the New Testament. The enlightening philosophy of the relationship between a human being and the Creator has led to the concept of universal human rights, although, the idea has been used to control other people, as much as it has been applied to liberate them.

Moral action becomes easy when one is armed with the actual knowledge of what is right, and what is wrong. This is only obtained of course, through your own real life experiences, because one can only "know" that which has been experienced. Belief, on the other hand, is something altogether different.

Right or wrong, true or not, is irrelevant to any belief system, because beliefs are often co-opted from indirect source material, and adopted to substitute for actual experience. Remember, morality has nothing to do with the laws that men write, even though there may be a small overlap with Natural Law, because even men understand the laws of creation.

The true knowledge and understanding of our world comes with having experienced things for yourself, and reflecting upon the occurrences and manifestation of things that come to pass. Only with this actual knowledge can you both recognize and tame your thoughts, along with the emotions that come with them, so that you may act with moral authority.

Acting with moral authority gives you an advantage in determining a resolution of the outcome. This does not mean you will necessarily emerge successful, and since in the battle of morality, the opposition is evil, there is a chance you might end up dead, or much worse. When you act with moral authority, though, you must indeed have it, not just proclaim it.

A willful force that is much stronger than all others is helping you to generate a just and desirable outcome. This is the power of the "Christ Consciousness" and the mastery of the Generative Principle that I have been discussing. All may possess this gift, if only they understood where it really comes from.

Chapter VI

Generating the Future

Living with an actual moral code has always been the key to maintaining a civilized society. One in which humans both prosper, and enjoy their brief existence on this earth. The problem we face, seems to be that to survive in this contrived excuse for a civil society, one must act almost universally without morals. We are taught to behave immorally, and are rewarded for participating in a system that is built upon a complete fabrication. A huge lie, that rationalizes the violence and coercion of the state, and produces enormous benefits to the ruling class through this system of human bondage.

This is the overwhelming, and catastrophic threat, that humanity faces at this current moment in time. The unjust system of economic slavery that has been foisted upon mankind, by the machinations of a few very wealthy and powerful families, must come to an end. It cannot stand, and will fall, regardless of how it does so. The results can be either disastrous, or exceptionally satisfying, depending upon how it's retired.

The undeniable truth of the Generative Principle is that there is no set future. All possible outcomes are in play until they are ruled out by the collapse of the wave function. With the probabilities of the actual outcome continually increasing, until the result is finally manifested as the current situation. The closer we get to creating an actual occurrence, the more effort is required to generate an alternative manifestation.

As you may have discovered during your time on earth, it is simply not possible to change what has already occurred, no matter how badly you may want to do so. Time is but a marker that the faculty of the mind bestows upon the generation of reality.

This reality is in a constant state of flux, and is forever changing, thus becoming the end results of our dreams and desires, and the moments in time that make up our existence. It will never cease in its infinite unfolding, and you cannot stuff it back into a bag.

What has occurred introduces the possibilities of what can occur next. Cause and effect can never be eliminated from this existence. It is indeed, the most obvious, and dominating principle, of Syncromysticism. We must make the proper choices, so that what has yet to occur, is effectively influenced by our powers of generation.

When one considers the momentum, or probability, of a future event occurring, they can then plan how to deal with such a situation. Should they stay at home and not bother with going to the parade, or just bring an umbrella? They must weigh numerous factors from their previous experiences. How accurate has the weatherman been in the past? What's to lose or gain either way? Many thoughts will flow through your head, and an uncountable number of previously generated and consequential effects, will come together and become a moment in your life, that you have tried to both, foresee, and willfully effect.

Some wise guy, once said, that making predictions was a risky proposition, especially if they're about the future. For some reason, though, the world is full of people who claim to be better suited than you, to do just this very thing. A quick reality check of past prognostications, demonstrates the futility of predicting a future that doesn't yet exist. Still, people want to know, and so long as there is a demand, there will always be a supply.

When we analyze the course of events, that continually drive cause and effect to generate the shifting manifestations we call reality, we find that we can't get to far along before the possibilities overwhelm us. We all want to have a better future, but just how much effort one must apply to affect a specific outcome, varies on an infinite scale.

Ordinary human beings, are just not informed enough about a variety of necessary knowledge that is crucial to the betterment of their lives. There isn't any reason why they couldn't be, they just aren't. Of course, you can be led by others, or purchase these services in exchange for your property, but they can never actually provide this knowledge to you, only help to direct your actions, if you choose to trust them. Now, if you have obtained any actual experience with putting your trust in others, then you surely know what a risky proposition that is, in and of itself.

The first thing one must do to participate in the generation of future events, is secure actual knowledge of universal mechanics. Of course, these truths are fundamental to the transcendental knowledge of the Eternal Consciousness. Of which you are a unique, and infinite point of view. A lens of perception into the generating Cosmos. This is the symbolism of the "All Seeing Eye"

The knowledge and ability inherent to the mind, is used to form the foundation in the act of perception. This is the true Spirit, an infinite division of the Eternal Consciousness. The originating source of "The All." The Divine Spirit and Creator of all things, is not watching you, it sees the act of creation through you.

Your place in the food chain is irrelevant to the powers that categorize the experience of a willful creature. As a human being, you may not need to get a degree in theoretical physics, to become a successful practitioner of mysticism, but a basic understanding of physical sciences, and a good knowledge of human behavior and historical remembrance, is necessary for you to assert your control over the unfolding future.

You must then come to recognize the existence of your own consciousness. Modern science has failed here, and is spreading a disingenuous narrative of a material reality that reduces the power of the Spirit down to a convenient illusion. One must reject the idea, that the consciousness that they are experiencing is the result of a confluence of physical interactions.

All creatures engage the physical universe, with their own innate abilities to categorize and define reality. They then incorporate these experiences into knowledge and understanding based upon their own perspectives, and develop an independent identity, one that is separated from the unity of everything else.

Once you recognize your abilities to make sense of the world through your inherent powers of logic and reason, you begin to free your mind. The shackles of ignorance, foisted upon you, by those whom wish to control you, fall from your mind, like lead balloons.

You are now free to increase and hone these abilities, and to recognize that the situations that generate future occurrences, are being effected by the decisions that you are making. Once the momentum of an occurrence can be recognized by the observer, then, and only then, do you have any actual chance, of generating the favorable outcome which you desire.

This ability is of course an inborn and unalienable property of the mind, and is realized in every action, from grasping the existence of physical objects, to determining what these objects are, can do, and how they relate to your existence.

Your mind, acting with information derived through sense perception, observes objects that exist in space, over time, and then makes summary judgements about those objects. This is the only type of empirical evidence of the physical universe that we can quantify.

With the transcendental powers of the mind, bestowed upon it through the Eternal Consciousness, and an identity that perceives itself as completely independent, a living creature can now make decisions that affect the future existence of itself, and these objects. Depending upon the size and scope, of your knowledge and power, and combined with the circumstances that have generated your identity, any outcome that does not directly contradict the laws of physical phenomena, and conceptual continuity is possible.

Essentially you have the power to see into the future, and to alter the coming condition of the physical universe. All physical actions must have consequences, this is the law of the empirical sciences. Yet, a thought might not lead to any action, or consequences at all. If the effect of your actions is responsible for even the tiniest defined alteration, and the scientific method proclaims that it must, then you have willfully engineered the outcome of reality. The mind is truly superior to the matter with which it creates.

Obviously, your present mindfulness is going to determine how well you can affect the course of your own existence, and possibly many others. How far into the future can you see? Well, of course, that varies from person to person, and is also dependent upon how much experience they have in these sorts of things. Still, the main point cannot be disputed, the skill or ability that you display in any activity, demonstrates that one must visualize future moments, before they happen, if they wish to operate functionally in a changing environment.

Somehow, though, the power to see into the future is believed to be supernatural, or extraordinary. The ability to predict the outcome of probable events has frustrated anyone and everyone that has ever

attempted to do so. This of course leads to the false assertion that we cannot see into the future. An assertion that we have just established is itself not possible.

It is the lack of accuracy that disappoints our expectations of precognition. When you consider all the possibilities of a future moment in time, and all the variable factors that intertwine to produce the predicted outcome, the confluence of events that is going to produce your prognostication, must be nearly identical, and thoroughly inclusive of the ones that you anticipated, or it will be noticeably different then your description. Accuracy in the art of foretelling the future, is indeed, a very tricky concept, and this is what really separates the prophets from the prognosticators.

It is far easier to be accurate when the movements of the principle causes are cyclical, and dominating. A cyclical generator moves within a defined pathway. Your ability to judge the motion of objects in space, that are changing over time, allows for the recognition of patterns. The recognition of patterns allows you to anticipate opportunity and intervene timely. Thus, you can influence the cycle, or benefit from opportunistic situations facilitated by these cyclical motions.

Effectually, your conscious and willful intervention, or timely actions, are generating the positive future you anticipated, envisioned, and are moving towards.

The most obvious example of this ability as humans put it to work is Astrology. Not the fortune telling aspect that some humans fancy, but the actual ability to infer logic by observation of the heavens. These are the cyclical motions that take place consistently, and repeatedly. They affect the lives and livelihoods of all creatures, great and small. You may have no actual ability to affect the motions of these celestial bodies, but you are now in position to take advantage of the conditions they bring.

Any weather site or informational medium will post the time of tomorrows' sunrise, along with other information, such as tidal times and weather forecasts. The fact that the exact time of sunrise on any given day can be forecast in advance demonstrates our ability to accurately predict the future. This forecast is extremely accurate, because the momentum of the cyclical motions is of such tremendous force, that the probability of the expected outcome is near certain, although, it most definitely is not guaranteed. There are things that could take place terrestrially, or on a celestial scale, that would change or disrupt the momentum of even planets and stars, thus rendering our predictions inaccurate.

Observation of the heavens has given humanity much to think about since we first noticed the light of the moon. Something that obviously occurred well before any higher order logic, such as mathematics or philosophy. The light of the moon, or the absence of it, is one of the most obvious examples of how the position of celestial bodies can either benefit, or hamper your endeavors. Creatures great and small, recognize the cycles of it, and moderate their behavior accordingly.

We all understand that knowledge of the future gives us the ability to plan for and influence the future. No longer must you behave in a reactionary manner towards unanticipated factors that produce unexpected outcomes. Armed with the knowledge of what will eventually occur, you are now poised to use the circumstances of the approaching conditionality to your own advantage.

This type of knowledge may be only a limited understanding of a universal mechanism, but it can allow for immense increases in productivity and subsistence. Understanding these types of conditions, and the laws that govern their behavior, allows for the implementation of agriculture, warfare, and navigation, along with the development and usage of technology, so this is no small advantage.

Naturally, those who understand and profit from this knowledge are not exactly eager to share it with you. It is up to you to seek out the machinations of existence, that have been observed, measured, and defined, as one of many distinct phenomena.

Once you have obtained this valuable knowledge, then you can exercise your own ability to understand these natural cycles, and not just describe them. For description alone, is the singular role of science, and the mysteries of the universe, cannot be understood through empirical observation, by itself.

You should already know, that describing phenomena is wholly different from understanding phenomena. Empirical knowledge is insufficient for explaining the reasons that such things exist at all. Of course, the fall back defensive position for this inadequacy is the pronouncement that there is no purpose. This isn't however just a reactionary position of defensive scientists, it is an instituted policy of deception, that corrupts the entire academic and political institutions of modern science.

Rather than admit to the limitations of empirical evidence, and acknowledge that other tools and methods of inquiry are essential, in any effort to explain the phenomena of physical reality, and indeed, the existence of the universe itself. The modern scientific establishments of academic, and institutionalized oversight, continue to support a view of universal phenomena that is incoherent with what we observe.

Using the abilities of the mind to observe and categorize experiences of physical reality not only helps us to understand the world we live in, it is the basis of determining the limitations of our own existence. We know that the true self (The thinking thing defined by Descartes) exists within, and is dependent upon, the material aspects we observe and quantify through sense perception and mental examination.

We then use the knowledge of this empirical evidence as the basis of all scientific theory. One must understand, though, that this is not the only ability that our minds possess. The mystic understands the powers of the mind are independent of the phenomena which they observe, while at the same time knowing the physical phenomena that we witness, can never be independent from our own observations.

All empirical evidence of physical reality is affected by your point of view. This is indeed the profound lesson of relativity, and demonstrates to me, that Einstein was more of a philosopher than a scientist.

The reproduction of results, and demonstrations of predictability, are the real proofs of empirical understanding, yet, as I mentioned previously, they fail to explain why such restrictions and universal dictates should exist at all. Science alone can never answer the most important questions of existence, which are of course, why are we here, and how did we get here?

Now if you are one of these modern materialists, who believes that, somehow, scientists are the new universal authorities, you would just accept their aggrandized pronouncements as the absolute truth. That is until they turn around, shortly thereafter, and tell you how wrong they really were. At this point you may begin to doubt their conclusions. Which is why they often stick to their obviously falsified theories, until the next generation of people arises, and will accept the new more accurate descriptions as progress, without diminishing the scientists.

Many scientific theories, and scientists, have been ostracized and ridiculed by institutional "authorities," only to later have their observations canonized as the new basic understanding of the way things work. Science is never settled, provided your description can be more specific.

Sometimes the turn around on the advancement of empirical knowledge is sudden, and at other times, it can take centuries to move away from widely held perceptions. Let us look at the almost universally accepted, and almost sacred, theory of evolution through natural selection.

As far I am concerned this theory has been wholly discredited. Not the evolution part, everything evolves, cars, planes, cities, ideas, and even understanding, this my friends, is a function of time, and a consequence of willful desire. The discredited part is the idea that this evolution is blind, a complete accident, driven on only because inadvertent mutation, endows certain species to gain a significant advantage over a competing species, by being better equipped in a challenging environment.

As living creatures, containing their own unalienable connection to the Divine Spirit, and of course, access to the universal consciousness, the evolution of life is driven by the powers of the Creator, and by the desires of the creatures, that are now manifested as physical beings.

Generated by the consequences of thought in the mind of the Eternal Consciousness, each sentient being retaining a connection to the transcendental powers of the universal mind, then applies them in the act of perception, so that it may determine its new unique perspective, which thus enables it to form its own identity.

Bound to a material existence, the creature no longer sees the universe as it truly exists. It is now wholly dependent upon the circumstances that has generated its incarnation. As a defined, and limited creature, it can take full advantage of the physical environment that it is immersed within, while exploiting all opportunities that arise within the biological ecosphere. However, it is still limited in its existence by the consequences that generated it into a physical organism.

The advancement of technological investigation, and the consequential growth of archeological, and biological sciences, have not advanced the theory of evolution, even slightly, in the one hundred and fifty plus years since its inception. In fact, modern science has only damaged the notion of natural selection.

How has this theory been so damaged? Mostly through the continued advancements and understanding of genes, but also through the failure to discover transitional species in the fossil record. I'm going to give Darwin a pass on this one. He lived a long time ago, and the theory does make logical sense, but sometimes things are not what they seem to be. Another mark in his favor, is that he also conceded, that missing links in the fossil record would have to be found, to vindicate his theory. It's likely, that even he, might have misgivings about the theory today.

The main problem that empirical evidence has presented for the theory of evolution through natural selection, is in the act of mutation. A mutation is defined as an unintended error, a change that has arisen which produces a deviation to the desired form. As technology has become more advanced, and we can better analyze the chemicals and compounds that make up the genetic code, we have gained a new perspective on the role of DNA.

Specifically, and experimentally, it can be clearly shown through genomic sequencing, and through empirical observation, that mutations are almost always detrimental to the organism that experiences them, and that much effort and energy is expended by living organisms to repair and correct genetic errors, before they lead to the propagation of unwanted physical deformities.

You may think that this is no big deal, obviously, mutations take place, and some must be beneficial. Truthfully, it's more like some mutations are not detrimental to the creature. Of course, there may be some that can be beneficial in certain circumstances, but the odds of it being so beneficial, that the functions and operations of the pre-mutated species will be negated, approaches nil.

When you consider that the most advanced and superior organism on this planet (A Human Being) is the only one that isn't evolved to survive in its own natural environment, you must begin to seriously doubt the belief that accidental advantages in survivability drive evolution.

What has become clear, thanks to the evolving and developing understanding of our own human genome, is just how much of the genetic information that is contained in our DNA is inactive. It's essentially just a store of information that is accessible to our own consciousness.

The field of epigenetic research has shown that under certain environmental, physical, and mental conditions, we are able to activate our dormant genes, so that we may generate previously unexpressed physical traits and behaviors that will help us to achieve what had been previously beyond our abilities. This is empirical evidence for the existence of telekinesis.

As a thinking being, you understand that what motivates your actions, are your desires. You go after what you want. You find ways, and invent means, that move you towards the things that you long for. The mystic understands the universal commonality of the mental faculties, and can apply the same motivational theories to other living things, regardless of their standing in the hierarchy of the food chain.

When life crawls out of the sea onto the land, it does so because it wants something on that land. It desires to achieve some goal, and produces through its own understanding and capabilities, methods to succeed in its endeavors. Modern science has previously held the position that your genetic material solely determines your form and functions. The new understanding of epigenetics, is that the mind, a conscious awareness generated from the union of the spirit with the physical universe, controls the operation of the organism entirely, willfully activating or deactivating specific genetic information and abilities.

This is of course all done on a subconscious level, just the same as almost all your other bodily functions. "You," are more than just the spirit that drives the manifestation of your physical existence. You have become a part of something that is much more dependent upon the situations and experiences you are partaking in. This is the act of "being." You have now become a human "being" that resides in, and is wholly interwoven and dependent upon, the developing ecosystems of this physical plain, where we now find ourselves.

The mystic likes to differentiate between the spirit and the soul. We all contain the spirit within us, at our very core it drives us to create the world we now inhabit. A direct conduit to the universal mind, the spirit is the source of all creativity in the universe. The three innate powers of the spirit: telekinesis, telepathy, and the power of generation, intertwine with the physical universe, to create all the magnificent life forms that inhabit our world, and most certainly countless others.

When the spirit becomes bonded to the physical world, the resulting reflection of itself as distinct, and separated from creation, becomes the identity that we call the soul. A creature unable to differentiate between what you have now become, and what you truly are, is the outcome of this divine union.

Your existence is now best described as a point of view of the Divine Spirit. It is with you always, seeking to shape creation for its own reasons, and working through the efforts of all living things to achieve this goal. This does not mean, however, that all these things are acting in unison.

Each life form acts on its own behalf, using the powers bestowed upon it through the Divine Spirit, to achieve its needs and desires. Of course, there is a certain commonality in the essential necessities and desires of all living things, so if the Divine Spirit is at the core of all souls, then deep down inside we all really want to do the same thing, and that is to create.

What we create, and how we go about achieving it, depends on the materials we are working with, and the situations that arise, either intended, or consequentially. Obviously, the type of life we witness here on Earth cannot manifest itself in dissimilar universal environments, but that does not mean that those environments are devoid of life. A sentient life form may even be so alien to us, that we might not even recognize it, or comprehend the environment that it subsists within.

How long did it take humanity to discover the microscopic world that permeates our planet and ourselves? Is it possible that we ourselves are akin to the micro-organisms that inhabit and make up our own physical being? Can it be, that the Sun is the heart of a creature generated upon another plain of existence? Could the things that we perceive as stars and planets be manifested as atomic, and molecular structures, in an alternate universe? Well, the answer to all these questions, according to the Syncromystic principle of Correspondence, is yes. Simply stated, the concept of Correspondence is, "As above so below."

You are the deity of the micro-universe that is the trillions of cells and micro-organisms that your human form consists of. While these cells are not cognizant of the challenges, and situations, that you strive to deal with on a day to day basis, they maintain a degree of awareness that is suitable to the level that they must operate upon. It only follows then, that we could have no conception of the environment, or reality of the supreme deity, whom we refer to as "The All"

We still maintain a perceivable connection with the cells that make up our own bodies. Feelings of pleasure or pain, indicate to us, that important interactions amongst the countless numbers of cellular entities, are taking place, and may require some type of conscious intervention on our part. While science believes these signals and indications of bodily conditions are strictly mechanical, the mystics and other enlightened thinkers have shown that such systems can be highly affected or even completely controlled through concentrated mental processes.

You have probably heard this referred to as "mind over matter", and it has been demonstrated by many, in almost every known culture, since time immemorial. Even hypnotism is a path by which humans seek to gain control over our subconscious impulses and defenses.

The mystic rightly regards the mind as the supreme power of the Cosmos, and acts accordingly to impose their own powers, as limited as they may be, to successfully generate a future that is desirable to the self.

Chapter VII

The Practicing Mystic

So just how does one practice Syncromysticism? What must we do to expand and develop our mental powers, and how do we unleash our own mystic potential? Is it necessary to worship the Creator?

There are many questions that anyone should ask, when trying to understand or practice any religion at all. Most people, however, never ask any truly pertinent questions concerning their own religion. This is simply because they were born into it, and raised from a child to practice the faith of their parents. Remember, your very soul is the sum of all the accumulated experiences the spirit has known, as an incarnated being.

 The spirit may save the soul, if it fancies its reflection. This imitation of the original creation takes place in numbers that can only be described as infinite. Everywhere, and on unending plains of disparate realities. The omnipresent energy that is manifested into a defined physical experience, is available for all to use throughout the realms of existence.

The illusions of physical reality take place both above and below this plain of manifestation. The energy that surrounds them all is truly the

Eternal Consciousness. It cannot be defined. You are a part of it, and so you too cannot be defined. But your experience can be.

The desire to know is responsible for the generation of the infinite possibilities. One must question and examine the world in which they perceive themselves, if they are to understand their experience. Wherever they find themselves, the universal principles of conscious generation will apply to their experience.

The things that I have told you are all true, but you can never know this, unless your own experiences lead you to that conclusion. You might believe me, many have faith in the integrity of subjects they know little about, but there is nothing wrong with maintaining your own skepticism, in matters that are not, readily, apparent to you.

The principles of Syncromysticism are there to help you define the experience you are having, and to understand your connection in the unity of "The All." If you wish to practice mysticism for yourself, then there are a few more things you need to know.

Firstly, and most definitely, there is nothing inherently evil in the practice of mysticism. Yes, it is true, there are dark arts. Such is the nature of the duality, and there are consequences for employing sinister forces. The only powers you will be wielding, however, are those bestowed upon you by the Creator, and always with the Love that stacks the deck in your favor. Genuine thoughts of caring, that are amplified by the correspondence of the Creators love for the Cosmos.

Another important part of practicing mysticism is getting to know the truth. Of course, as I stated previously one cannot truly "know" anything, unless they have direct experience with the things they wish to know. Certainly the "All Truth" is unknowable to us as we exist in this world, but it is possible to understand what is true, and to use this knowledge to uncover greater truth as we progress in the journey towards our own enlightenment. How is this possible?

To put it simply, the truth, and by that, I mean any truth, even something such as a simple fact, never contains contradictions within itself, or with any other known truth. If a contradiction between two concepts recognized as supposed truths cannot be reconciled, then one or both must be cast aside as a falsehood. While this may be one of the basic rules of deductive reasoning, and is the fundamental rule of elementary logic, it is seldom put into practice by the average modern human.

Most human beings believe, or have come to accept, countless things that are in direct contradiction to each other, without ever giving such matters a second thought. Normally this doesn't occur until after early childhood, as it is noted that children observe and categorize all things anew, into their own understanding of what exactly is going on here. This is the reason why adults are often stunned at the wisdom and pronouncements of what we believe to be an inexperienced child. These children do not disregard their own observations and instinctual conclusions so easily. Normally, this doesn't occur until they have their own common sense restrained through formalized education.

Buried somewhere deep inside our own subconscious, we all possess an understanding of the world, that is based upon the totality of the actual situations that we have experienced, and have come to know through this experience. This may include things that we were taught in school, or told by others, if we have put this information into direct actions, and experienced the results for ourselves.

It is certainly true that one can be educated about things that they haven't yet experienced, or may never get the chance to experience. These things however will ultimately remain only beliefs to them, until they can undertake the necessary experiences that convert these limited understandings into knowledge.

One could certainly refute any teachings or concepts if they contradict what you know to be true. Again, knowing because you have actual knowledge through experience. It is far easier to dismiss a situation or concept, if it contradicts your known experiences in the matter. Such premises can be dismissed quite easily. It is far more difficult to ascertain what can be done, especially if you are not familiar with the limitations and possibilities of consequence.

If someone says they know who discovered America they are lying, but it has been taught as factual for hundreds of years. Having a good knowledge of recorded history, can help you narrow down a descriptive answer about the discovery of America that is true, although, obviously less definitive than previously expressed. Why claim a specific person discovered the land you inhabit anyway? You should know that it is done for a reason. Mysticism plays an enormous role in the mass perception of society and civilizations.

Practicing Syncromysticism requires you to know what is true, not everything that is true, but to perceive what is true about any experience you are partaking in. To the best of your abilities, of course. You must also, never discard, or subjugate, your own knowledge of truth to justify any conclusion. Keep in mind that we are talking about "Truth" here, and not mere facts.

An objection to this fundamental requirement, is the argument of subjective truth. If we can only know things by direct experience, then surely our knowledge must be limited to only the things that we ourselves have experienced. If that is true, then we cannot learn through research and academic instruction. While this is a valid argument and possibly a very good point, it misses the mark of truth, because it only focuses on specific and limited examples of experience.

The ability to categorize specific examples into broader classifications or situations, in conjunction with the basic principles that correspond to all manifestations of physical reality, allows us to judge how truthful the information we are receiving through second and third hand sources really is, but only if you know the limitations and the possibilities of the concept being expressed.

You may still be correct about a given situation or informational statement, even if you don't really know firsthand. Just because you may have never experienced something exactly similar for yourself, doesn't necessarily make your informed understanding about the subject incorrect. What really counts is how much weight you are going to give specific information regarding a dependent conclusion.

Let me use the well known and culturally popular game of baseball as an example of this point. If one picks up a newspaper and reads the sports scores from last night, they would have little reason to doubt that the information they received was untruthful or incorrect. While it's true that they couldn't know for sure, and in fact the information relayed may be incorrect, the benign and uncontroversial nature of reporting the results of ball games, relieves one from having to express cynicism or doubt about the reports.

Now it's still true that you don't really know for sure if the Blue Jays did beat the Yankees, or if the posted score is the correct one. You probably do, however, know something of the game itself, and the profession of baseball. Your interest in wanting to learn the outcome of the contest is driven by your knowledge and connection to the sport. You have most likely had a situational experience, that encompasses the concepts relayed to you by the box score in the morning paper.

There are other factors including technical errors of production, that may lead to a false or inaccurate result being reported, but your knowledge would certainly alert you if the reported score was a number impossible to attain, such as: Blue Jays 2, Yankees -1. If the game being discussed was football, then based upon your knowledge of that game, a score of Giants 1, Cowboys 0, would alert you to the falsehood, or mistake. This is what I define as contradictions of known truth.

Your direct experience with these sports, and the methods of reporting and publishing, allows you to safely incorporate the given information into your factual knowledge of the sport. If the information is incorrect, this in no way limits your knowledge and understanding of the concept, it is only a very specific, and minor instance of circumstance, of which you are in error of awareness. Adjustments can be made, and the correct results can be incorporated directly into your worldview quite easily, because such matters are inconsequential to your understanding of the concept of baseball. Remember, facts may be true, but facts are not "Truth."

Suppose you were witnessing a baseball game at the actual ballpark where it is being played. A runner hits a ground ball to the third baseman, and with your perfect vantage point, you observe him beat the throw to first base. The umpire calls him out. What now is the truth of this matter? It is given that your eyes witnessed the event clearly and accurately. If you say that he was safe, then that is not true. The rules of the game implicitly state that the umpire makes the determination about his status. If you read the newspaper the next day, the box score will read that he grounded out on a throw from the third baseman, that is a fact.

You could of course describe the situation more accurately, and remark how he clearly beat the throw to first base, but was called out by the umpire anyway. Now you have stated the truth, and you "know" the truth, because you have experienced it, but if you argue with your friend the next day, and the whole of your statement is that he was safe, then your pronouncement is surely false.

Within topics of complex situations, or instances of incomplete information, you might never be able to know the actual truth of what has occurred, or is taking place. That is why when one attempts to understand something by applying the scientific method, they must demonstrate empirically that their conclusions are valid. Without this important method of confirmation, any scientific theory at all is to be sincerely doubted.

The skepticism of undemonstrated conclusions has almost totally disappeared from our modern culture. It has been replaced by the monopolization of corporate institutions, and the sanctioning of academic elitists. Statements and conclusions are taken completely on faith alone, provided the presenter is accredited by these institutions. In the age of information, the possession and dissemination of ideas and concepts, is ruthlessly controlled and managed by those, whom seek to exploit real knowledge for their own financial and political advantage.

In fact, it isn't impossible to attain an accurate understanding by incorporating well documented and proven information, and non-contradictory concepts into your own worldview. Theories must remain exactly that, while demonstrable scientific descriptions, and actionable technologies should be taken as factual experience.

Even if you don't really understand how the airplane flies, you can see that it does. Knowing that Galileo's experiments with falling objects can be, and have been duplicated many times, allows you to accept their validity, even if you do not wish to perform them yourself. There just isn't any reason to believe anything, or anyone, if their pronouncements contradict your own actual experience in those situations.

When you begin to trust in your own ability to determine what is really happening, then you can act on your "gut feelings", and cultivate your instinctual behavior to ensure more positive outcomes in your personal endeavors. This is how you practice mysticism. You take control of the Magic that is the force of Creation, and break the spell of the dark arts that bind the minds of mortal men.

Some of the clearest examples of actual knowledge, and instinctual behaviors, triumphing over superior ability and force, are to be witnessed in the world of professional sports. The crafty veteran who has witnessed, and been involved in many types of situations, uses his experience to defeat superior athletic ability. This person is taking advantage of the situation instinctively, leveraging the type of knowledge that is only attainable through direct experience.

A seasoned contender makes use of factors and situational moments that are very difficult to quantify in mere words. The subconscious mind, working underneath your current level of interests, has classified all experience under the categories by which it has perceived your entire existence.

Without defining the current situation that you find yourself experiencing, and using words that are unsatisfactory for the occasion, or concepts that take too much time for you to analyze. A person can understand the opportunities and possibilities presented to them, and go with their gut instincts to take advantage of a less experienced opponent. One that does not possess the situational awareness, that only comes from instantaneous recognition of an infinite number of specific scenarios.

There is, of course, so much more to understanding anything than book learning and academic definitions can impart upon anybody. This does not mean, however, that proven standards and practices should be ignored. Principles and values should be given priority when your decisions are made and implemented. Too many times slick politicians, and academic proponents of confiscatory behavior, justify the outright theft of peoples' property, and the murder of innocent people, through the rationalization of a "greater good."

Putting principles above your behavior allows you to understand that a system that is based upon wrongful conduct can never produce a positive and successful outcome for its participants. The ends never justify the means. If the means are corrupt, or reprehensible, then the imposition of the means begin to outweigh the benefits of the ends, and so the means, become the ends, in this unbalanced equation.

Having been born into a system that is absolutely corrupted by political alliances and big money influences, it is hard to understand just how wrong it all is. It all seems perfectly normal, doesn't it? They make the laws and you obey them. Of course, they don't put it that bluntly, if they did, you would surely rethink your participation in the scheme of things. At the very least, you would be more open to reforming this monstrosity we call government.

They work diligently to obfuscate your subjugation with political charades, and institutionalized indoctrination through public education. Repeatedly telling you, it's a government by the people, and for the people, but then assuring you, that the laws need to be interpreted by "specially appointed," and learned officials.

The truth is, that in an honest system no one is above the law. The courts do not have a right to interpret clearly defined statutes, and regulations. The Constitution stands supreme, and if judges rule against what is clearly spelled out in the documents, it is your duty to have them removed through the political process defined under the law.

Again, the main problem here is that the public has abandoned the values and principles that ensure their own freedoms. It is wrong to take peoples possessions without their direct consent. Any practicing mystic understands this, and is opposed to any argument that justifies consent through a social contract, or implied consent through political participation.

Although we can't just destroy the system that oppresses us, we can stop it from becoming even more powerful, and then begin dismantling it through more honest and liberal legislation. The system must not be rooted in, or dependent upon, the monopoly of violence and coercion, of which, all modern governments are founded.

This doesn't mean that you need to refuse to pay your taxes and be forced into a cage at the point of a gun. You simply must recognize that the system is corrupt, and oppose all measures that that seek to further empower the government at the expense of the citizenry. Support and champion all efforts to diminish the "authority" of the state and return power to the people, by reaffirming the limitations of our unique constitution, which binds governmental powers.

Freedom demands vigilance. When you are actively involved in addressing the issues that are important to yourself, your family, and your community, you have a measure of control over our collective prosperity, or enslavement.

One must weigh all the choices they make, and visualize how those decisions will manifest through the laws of cause and effect. The outcome or consequences of your decision need not be immediately apparent to you, or anyone else, for them to be a factor in the causation of future consequences. If the seed has been planted, then we shall reap what we sow.

Now some may doubt this is mysticism at all. Others may believe it to be Karma, or blowback, or just plain civic responsibility. In fact, it is all these things. Yet, the art of Syncromysticism does require you to take meaningful physical actions in concert with your enlightened consciousness. All actions are born in thought. The cause and effect of physical reality is always driven on by our conscious desire to shape our reality.

Any effort to achieve a desired outcome requires a thoughtful plan of action if it is to succeed. When that plan diminishes the freedoms and natural rights of others, it faces a high probability of failure, due to the consequences and operations of Natural Law.

When we engage in honest and righteous behavior the probability of success is amplified by the desired outcome of collective consciousness. There is, absolutely, a plan for the continued advancement of life experiences, and a progression intended to achieve mastery of the physical universe, while still retaining awareness of our spiritual origins.

Life continues to evolve and advance in whatever capacity that it can, and in any physical conditions that it may use to facilitate its creative endeavors. There are universal laws that govern the behavior of both physical matter, and of conscious choices, but one must act if they wish to create.

You only need to realize the consequences of putting your thoughts into actionable motion, to practice this considerate and righteous behavior. Of course, this requires that you have learned and understood the reasons that you exist, and the previous consequences that have brought you to your current situation.

Knowledge of historical experiences and physical sciences, must be obtained and practiced by humanity at large, if we are to achieve success in our common undertaking. Failure to recognize and implement a plan of action towards this goal will result in disaster and the ultimate extinction of humanity.

There are of course many human beings that are working towards commendable goals without understanding the mystic aspects of creative generation, but their efforts are hindered, because they often wish to implement a means to an end that defies the tenants of Natural Law. Such methods are bound to enact the Karmic consequences that will ensure their miserable failure.

With a recognition of Natural Law and the principles of Syncromysticism spelled out within this treatise, humanity can further evolve into a higher order species. One that can achieve almost any possible future, and begin to explore the universe at large, with advanced technological solutions, for both a physical exploration of the galaxy, and a metaphysical examination of the essence behind our manifestation as conscious entities.

Printed in the USA
CPSIA information can be obtained
at www.ICGtesting.com
LVHW021025300824
789721LV00009B/300